# Dumb Dog

By Margaret Beames

Illustrated by Mario Capaldi

DOMINIE PRESS
Pearson Learning Group

Publisher: Raymond Yuen
Project Editor: John S. F. Graham
Editor: Bob Rowland
Designer: Greg DiGenti
Illustrator: Mario Capaldi

Text Copyright © 2003 Margaret Beames
Illustrations Copyright © 2003 Dominie Press, Inc.
All rights reserved. No part of this publication may
be reproduced or transmitted in any form or by any
means without permission in writing from the publisher.
Reproduction of any part of this book, through photocopy,
recording, or any electronic or mechanical retrieval system,
without the written permission of the publisher, is an
infringement of the copyright law.

Published by:

### Dominie Press, Inc.

1949 Kellogg Avenue
Carlsbad, California 92008 USA

www.dominie.com

1-800-232-4570

Paperback ISBN 0-7685-1820-2
Printed in Singapore by PH Productions Pte Ltd
  2 3 4 5 6 PH 05

# Table of Contents

Chapter One
**Badger Dog** ...................................................... 5

Chapter Two
**A Sausage Roll** ................................................ 10

Chapter Three
**You're Not Going** ........................................... 13

Chapter Four
**Off the Main Trail** .......................................... 18

Chapter Five
**Not-So-Dumb Dog** ........................................ 24

## Chapter One
# Badger Dog

Hello. My name is Fritz. My human called me that when I was just a puppy. She was very nice to me and fed me well, but she did not take me out very often. I have very short legs. I guess she thought I did not need much exercise.

Then my human got sick. She stayed in bed all the time. I was lonely. I watched the children going past the house. I wanted to go out and play with them, but the door was shut. After a while, a man came and took me away to a strange place with a lot of other dogs. I was in a kennel.

One day, a woman came. She looked at all the dogs. When she came to me she said, "Isn't he sweet?" Her voice was kind, and when she picked me up her hands were gentle.

She put me in her car, and soon we were driving away. I'd been adopted! I was a little nervous at first, but I was happy, too. I felt that something good was about to happen. When the car stopped and she lifted me out, something good did happen. There, running to meet us, was a young boy. I was going to have someone to play with! But something was wrong.

"What is that?" The boy said. He pointed at me and sounded angry.

"This is Fritz. He's a dachshund. Isn't he cute? Say hello to him, Scott."

"Aw, Mom!"

8

Now I knew their names—*Mom* and *Scott*. Scott picked me up and patted my head. That was good enough for me. I licked his nose.

"Yuck!" he said and wiped his face. He put me down a little roughly. "You call that a dog? I wanted a shepherd or a retriever, a real dog."

"*Dachshund* means *badger dog* in German," Mom told him. "Hunters used them to dig badgers out of their holes. They're brave little dogs."

I hadn't known that. I was a brave little dog! It made me feel proud.

"You'll grow to love him," Mom said.

"I don't think so," Scott muttered, but I wasn't worried now. I knew he'd like me when he got to know me. We could play some good games together. He would be my new human.

Chapter Two
# A Sausage Roll

Scott's friends came to see me—Trevor, Joe, and Dennis. They all stood in a circle around me.

Trevor said, "That's not a dog, it's a doorstop."

Joe said, "No, it's a sausage. Who

stuffed it, Scott?"

Dennis said, "Help! It's moving!"

They acted scared and ran away from me. "Save us!" they yelled. "We're being chased by a savage sausage!"

I galloped after them, barking, chasing them all around the garden. It was fun, but I was getting winded. I was too fat to go very fast. When we came to the edge of the lawn, I went tumbling over and over down a slope.

I picked myself up, wagging my tail. The boys were rolling around, laughing. "That's what you call a sausage roll!" they said.

"Dumb dog!" said Scott.

That became his name for me. Mom still called me Fritz, but to Scott I was Dumb Dog.

The boys jumped on their bikes and sped away. Scott went with them. I tried to follow, but they went too fast. I barked and barked, but they didn't stop.

Mom came out and picked me up. "Don't worry," she said. "He'll take you for a walk when he gets back."

## Chapter Three
# You're Not Going

Scott took me for a walk every day. "Do I have to, Mom?" he said. "He's so fat."

"He won't be fat if you walk him every day," Mom explained.

When we went out, Scott pulled his cap down over his eyes so you could hardly see his face. "Come on, Dumb Dog," he would say, "before anyone sees me."

After a few weeks of going for walks, I was able to run faster and farther than before. Scott's friends stopped laughing at me. We played some good games together. They even took me with them to most places. I could run along with them, even when they were on their bikes, if they went slow. But they didn't take me to a place called *school*. Dogs were not allowed there.

One day, I saw Scott take his bike out of the shed. I raced up to him, ready to go for a run.

Scott said, "Forget it, Dumb Dog. You're not going."

My ears went down. My tail went down. I tried to think if I'd done anything bad to make him angry. I didn't dig any holes

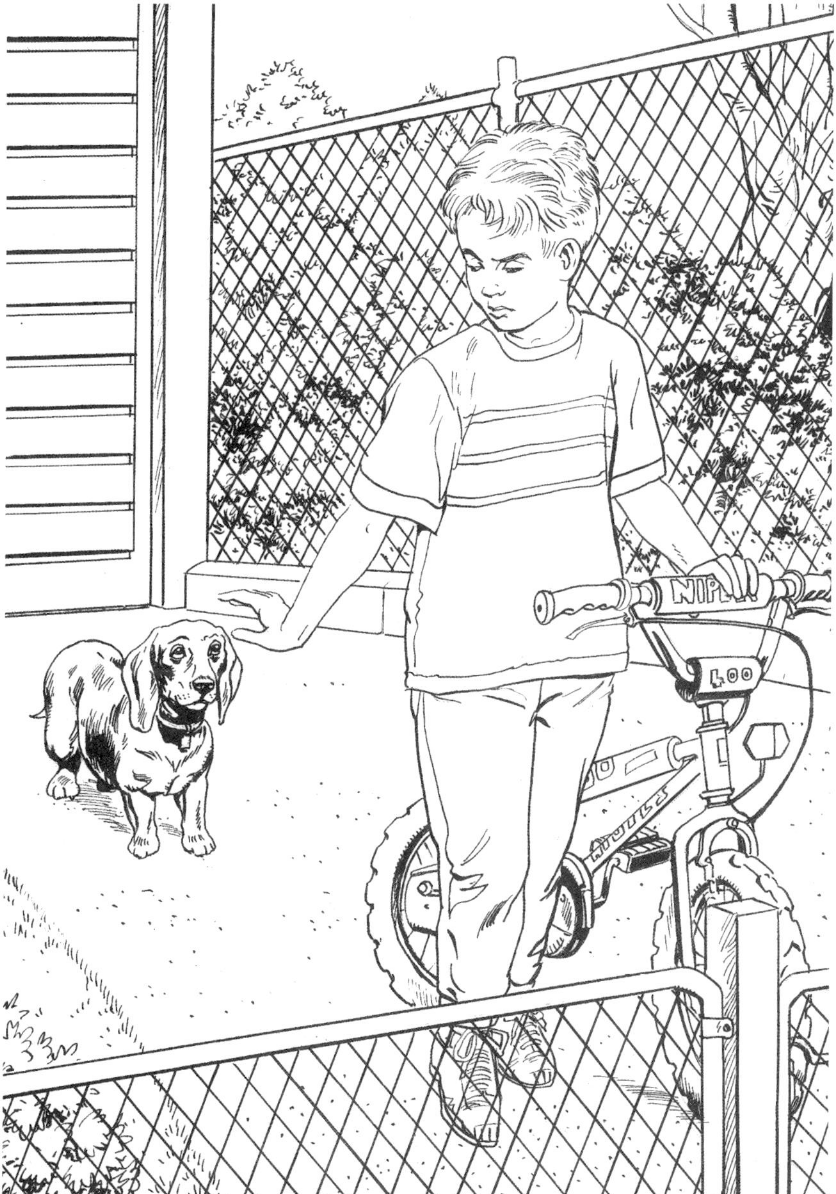

in the lawn. I didn't chew up any of his shoes. I left the laundry on the clothesline. I left the cat alone most of the day. I was a good dog.

Scott opened the gate, wheeled his bike out onto the sidewalk, and shut the gate again.

He looked back at me and shouted, "Stay, Dumb Dog, stay!"

I didn't know what that meant. It just made me more confused. I tilted my head to try and hear him better, but he didn't say anything else.

Then he jumped on his bike and pedaled away, alone. Why didn't he take me? I wanted to go, too. I jumped as high as I could, but I couldn't get over the gate. I'm not very good at jumping.

I'm good at digging, though. I put my paws into the ground, and soon dirt was flying in all directions. It did not take long before I had dug a hole under the fence big enough for me to wriggle through. I was out! I scampered off in the direction Scott had taken.

I couldn't see him. It's hard to follow the scent of a bicycle, but I knew he was heading toward the river. And I knew the way because I'd been there before.

Chapter Four
# Off the Main Trail

When I came to the river, I couldn't see Scott anywhere. I decided to sniff around a little. After a little while, I found his bike hidden in some bushes. Now that he was walking, it was easy to pick up his scent. I followed his trail through the trees.

The scent led me off the main trail, then back onto it, then off again. And then it stopped. I had lost it. I was puzzled. Where could he have gone without leaving a scent? I barked loudly. *Where are you?* I was asking.

"Fritz?" It was Scott's voice—and it was coming from a deep hole right beside me.

I peered down into it. What was he doing down there?

"Is that you, Fritz? Get back, you'll fall in, too," Scott called. "Home, Fritz, home! Get help. Go on, you dumb dog! Home!"

I wasn't going home without my human. I tried to get closer. Suddenly, the edge of the hole began to crumble and break. I started to slip. I tried to hold on, but the ground gave way. I fell into the hole. I wasn't hurt because Scott caught me. I'm not sure he meant to, because he gave a gasp and fell over with me on top of him. I was so happy to see him that I licked his face all over.

"Get off, you dumb dog!" he said. "Now we're both trapped, and no one knows where we are!" All the same, he hugged me so I knew he was glad to see me, too.

I could not understand why he was down there. It was just a deep hole with a long tunnel leading in both directions from it. It was cold and damp. We could have much more fun up above. He could climb trees and I could chase squirrels.

Something dropped onto Scott's face and he jumped up. "Yuck, bugs!" It was only a dead leaf, but I guess he could not see as well as I could in the dark. It was time to go, I decided. I could feel a cool wind blowing, so I started running toward it.

"Hey, wait for me! Fritz? Where are you?" Scott yelled.

I ran back to his side and he hugged me again. "Hey, don't do that, you hear?" he said. "Stay with me, OK?" He found a piece of string in his pocket and tied it to my collar.

I started running again. This time Scott came with me, holding tight to the string. It was very dark, even for me. Scott stumbled several times, but on the wind I could smell rabbits and river water and wood burning. Farther away, I smelled meat cooking. I started running faster.

I could hear Scott's hand brushing along the damp wall as he stumbled along beside me. "Wait up, Dumb Dog," he said. So I did.

Then I stopped completely. A wall of dirt and stones blocked the way. Scott sounded very unhappy. He gave a kind of growl. "Now we're really trapped," he said. "We'll have to go back. Maybe if I can yell loud enough someone will hear us."

Chapter Five
# Not-So-Dumb Dog

**H**e tugged at the string. "Come on, Dumb Dog," he said, but I could still feel the wind blowing across my nose. I dug my feet in and refused to go.

Then I started digging. The dirt was hard packed, but I kept at it. I put my

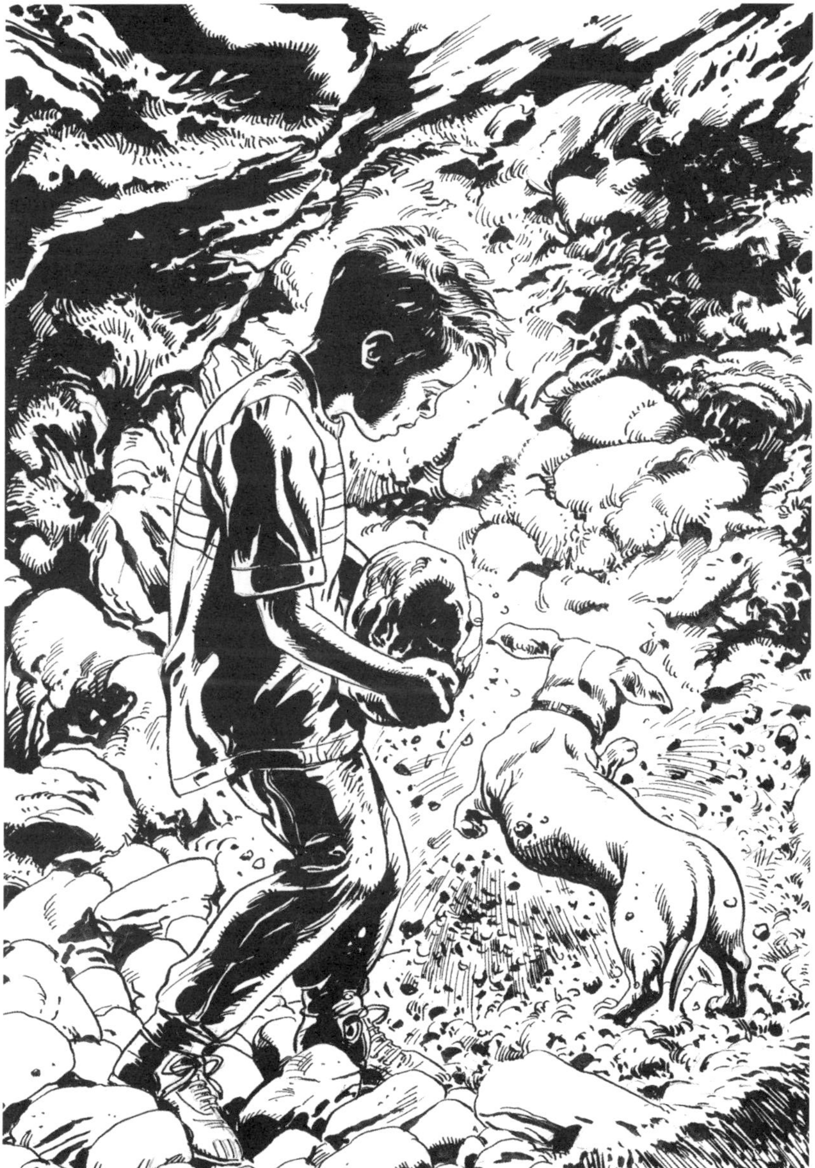

nose close to the ground where the wind blew strongest and sniffed. Then I dug faster.

Scott must have seen how hard I was working, because he began to help, lifting out the stones.

My paws were sore, and I think Scott's hands hurt, too. He said, "Ouch!" a couple of times, but we didn't give up.

Suddenly, the wall crumbled and there was a space just big enough for me to wriggle through. I was out! I barked for joy.

Then I heard Scott's voice. "Hey! What about me?" He was still in the tunnel! Of course, he's bigger than I am. I still had some work to do.

I dug furiously from outside, and Scott dug from inside the tunnel. At last he scrambled out on his hands and knees, covered with mud, but so happy to be out in the sunshine.

"Come on, Not-So-Dumb Dog," Scott said. "Now show me the way home."

That was easy. I led him back to the path. Before long, he found his bike, and we were on our way home.

Now Scott takes me with him everywhere he goes. I even ride in a basket on his bike. He still calls me *Dumb Dog*. It's his special name for me, and I can tell by the way he says it that he loves me. But no one else is allowed to call me anything but *Fritz*.